Poems To My Younger Self

Shanika Cuthbert

Presentation by *BookLeaf Publishing*

Web: www.bookleafpub.com

E-mail: info@bookleafpub.com

ISBN: 9789358319316

First edition 2023

To the little girl born in North Central Hospital in 1996. You have always been destined for greatness and this book is a proof of that. I love you Shanika Shannel Cuthbert.

ACKNOWLEDGEMENT

I extend my deepest gratitude, first and foremost, to my students who consistently asked, "Ms. Cuthbert, did you finish your book yet?" Finally, I can confidently respond, "Yes, I did, well, at least one of them." Special thanks to Ibrahim Sanogo for daily reminders to craft a poem, and to Ashraff and Gabe for their genuine interest in my work.

Heartfelt appreciation goes to Paula Ramos for touching my spirit and offering the right words to a young girl in need of belief. Mrs. Goldstein, my high school math teacher, deserves acknowledgment for the enduring smile she wore daily, and to Jill and Melissa Goldstein for their countless hours supporting my journey through an honors degree in English.

To my nieces—Shantell, Tamara, T'mya, and Chloe—your presence has fueled my aspiration to be great. To my beautiful sister Jody, I miss you daily; your regular check-ins and lessons on accountability remain cherished. Sammie, you've transcended friendship, becoming a sister. Kion, for being reliable, thank you.

Tameica, your lessons and prayers have left an indelible mark; Shev, thank you for letting me be heard; Daejon, I cherish having you as my brother. Patsy, for your stories, laughter, pain, and care during my ill days—thank you.

Khalid, your unhesitating welcome into your life speaks volumes. Amir, your bubbly spirit and reminder to be happy are invaluable.

Brother Garfield, for stepping up, being my dad, and not shying away from the truth—I am forever grateful and love you dearly.

Gary Tolan, your belief in the 14-year-old songwriter in me has left an everlasting impact; and Trevor, your belief in my talent shaped me during crucial moments. Screechy Dan, you have changed my life for the better.

A special nod to Jevvo for reigniting my love for music and to JB for the collaborative exploration of new sounds. Raymond, your encouragement, cheerleading, and constant reminders of my inner and outer beauty resonate deeply.

Trevine, your kindness in my darkest moments defines our sisterhood.

Daddy, thank you for still caring and calling. To my ancestors, your strength flows through my veins, and for that, I am grateful.

Thanks to my therapists, past and present; Brandon for listening and validating my experiences. Iris, Sarah, and Marie for the coping techniques and providing insightful homework.

To the doctors who aided my survival and recovery from Guillain Barre Syndrome and autoimmune disorders, my heartfelt gratitude.

To everyone who sent prayers and positive vibrations, thank you.

Conja, thank you for being a genuine friend, who always keeps me in mind. Spencer, your consistent love has brought endless smiles. Christian, your authenticity and unapologetic self have been a source of motivation.

Hana, witnessing your infinite love for Chris has been profound.

A special thank you to Classical Charter Schools for providing the opportunity to teach the smartest 3rd and 4th graders on Earth. Princeton, you've taught me unexpected lessons, and I am forever grateful for the endearing moments, whether being considered a "baddie," having locks of hair kept, or the student who professed love. Special mention to Stephanie and Sarah, the OG3, for showing grace during challenging days. I am forever grateful for you both.

Ree, your love and light is powerful.

Dinetra and Brittny, thank you for becoming friends who bring laughter. Marshella, your shoulder and support during difficult times have been invaluable.

To the Fantastic Four, trusting me as your manager is an honor. Jaribel, your team spirit makes me proud, and the friendly banter with Andy about who's the funniest brings me joy. Nicole, your words brighten my bad days. Frank, Jay, Zavon, Devon, Maria, Ariel, Marlaine, Meranda, Catherin, Dicoda—each of you has played a unique role in my journey, and I am grateful.

To the families of every scholar I've taught, your impact on my life is immeasurable. I firmly believe that "I needed them more than they needed me." Kevin, thank you for choosing my application and being on this classical journey with me. Adwoa, the way you spread your Black

Girl Magic is inspiring. To everyone who has contributed to my experience—thank you from the bottom of my heart.

Finally, a heartfelt acknowledgment to my dearest friend, Obie. Your steadfast support has been my anchor during challenging times. Your embodiment of unconditional love is truly exceptional and I wish everyone could experience it. If not in this lifetime, then hopefully the next, because you define happiness. Your positive influence has reshaped my perspective, proving we are more than the lives we are born into. You understand my moods, from joy to sorrow and everything in between. You recognize my qualities, and have encouraged me to embrace them. There is nothing wrong with being soft, strong, smart, funny, ambitious, classy and vulnerable. You ensure I recognize my worth, and I wish there was a scale to measure the magnitude of your value in my life.

PREFACE

I have been enamored with words my entire life. Even before I could form letters, I would take the paper from the packaging (half cardboard/half paper—I never knew exactly what to call it) left over when my mother bought a new pair of stockings for work, and just scribble away. I vividly recall presenting these scribbles to her, urging her to read my creations. It's safe to say that from an early age, I always sought constructive criticism. Then there was my imaginary teacher; I have no recollection of her, but I like to believe it was my grandmother (whom I never met but was also a teacher) showing me the ropes. Perhaps she sensed that I would someday follow in her footsteps. Who knows.

Writing initially entered my life in the form of song. Enthralled by music, I aspired to be like Alicia Keys—singing, writing, and playing the piano. Imagine my disappointment when 18-year-old me discovered she didn't write every song she sang (I know, I know). I never did learn how to play the piano, and I continue to sing to this day with every intention of being recognized as a global superstar. However, as the saying goes, "time is the master."

I have always known that I am a creative being. Others didn't quite understand it. Family members and 'friends' discouraged me from pursuing my dreams, consistently singing the same song about needing a sustainable job, a career that "can feed me." As an empath, I then convinced myself I could become a therapist or a psychiatrist. After all, they made a lot of money.

There I was at Port Richmond High School, listening to my sister tell Ms. Delaney about my desire to join the school's Medical Technology program. Ms. Delaney questioned me; she knew my heart wasn't in it, but I convinced myself otherwise. I had always wanted to help people, and since I couldn't do it through literature or music, this seemed like the next best thing. Then I met Ms. Ramos—the woman who affectionately called me "little Maya." She praised my poems as beautiful when I had never heard such words before. She uttered, "We need to get you published" and imparted the wisdom, "If you do what you love, the money will follow."

I never forgot that; I never forgot her. To this day, I live by that quote. If my body wasn't already at tattoo capacity (which is one), it would probably be inked somewhere visible. For now, it's etched into my heart and mind. I share this to encourage you to follow your dreams, disregarding the opinions of others, because you can be whatever you want in this life. With that being said, I hope you enjoy my poetry; I know Ms. Ramos will.

Would you believe

Oh dear little me,
Would you believe
That you're all grown up now?
Planting your seeds,
In the mind of the innocent,
They look up to you,
They were worth all the pain,
and heartache you went through

Your life was once snatched
From 2018
You regained control
Or so it may seem
You almost strayed
Had no self-esteem
But now you're a teacher
And the grass is still green

Oh dear little me,
Would you believe
They call you Ms. Cuthbert
But what does that mean?
Your word holds weight
So you must mind your tongue
For the words that you sing

Cannot be unsung
Just like the words that you say
cannot be undone

Your first week of school
There was a question proposed,
"Is God real?"
What careful words that you chose.
You said I believe,
you should go home and ask mommy or daddy.
Whatever they say,
sweet child, is the way

And from that day forth, you were aware
That it's beyond your hair and outfit they stare.

They stare in your eyes,
They notice frown lines
They notice your pitch, and the change in your
tone,
Or how they must hush when your doctor is on
the phone
They ask you questions,
"Is everything okay?"
And you will say yes,
And that is the price that you pay.
To preserve their young minds

You speak to their souls

You tell them you love them
In case they don't hear it at home.
You go hard,
You don't stop
Even when you're physically numb
Because those kids are your drive.

Oh dear little me,
Would you believe?
You're doing just fine.

Dinner at Gio's (A Haiku)

4

Dinner at Gio's
With Didi and Ree, I smile
They both feel like home.

Voices

Voices,

All at once, distorted

They keep going and going.

How convincing they can be.

And how cliche for me to say, IGNORE THEM.

Especially when it's easier said than done.

You're failing (no you're not)

You should've been someone else (You're exactly who you are meant to be)

You should've been married by now.

It's getting too late.

Your biological clock is starting to fade.

This is the end.

Your life isn't worth living.

You won't make it.

Because when has anything ever worked out in
your favor?

But YOU have to distinguish

Fact from fiction

Lust from a real connection

What's right

What's wrong

Trusting your gut

As if you're writing a new song

Cancel the noise

Without your AirPod Pros

Use your pen to save you

Write your poems and prose

Don't let them alter what is already known.

You are here for a reason

You survived it all

For a reason

Every tear that crawled across your face

Held meaning

Even the ones that detoured and landed right
under your nose

Those too had a purpose

To release,

to speak,

to the creator in a way that words couldn't.

To say I'm hurting, I'm in pain

Please just make it go away

One day… you will beat all those voices.

Black Men

Dear Black Men,
I love you.
I was taught to hate you
But my belief that you are one of the most
valuable creatures on Earth remains
unwavering.

Your skin is gold.
Your smile is my home.
Your laughter—rare
and happiness—forbidden

I want for you, everything I want for
Myself.
Love,
Abundance ,
Success,
Compassion,
Gratitude,
and Wisdom.

Despite the whispers you have heard.
You compliment us well. Allow me to give you
your flowers.
Embrace the credit, rightfully deserved.

To the leaders, providers, and protectors.
I appreciate you.
I value you.
I see you.
I thank you.

I can't imagine how hard it must be,
In a society where the color of your skin
Automatically means you're guilty.

If you cry, you are weak
And if you don't cry,
your feelings are a lie.

You can't win.

How many times have you sacrificed your
happiness for someone else?
How many times have you been compelled to say
"I'm good?" While feeling antithetical?

I know.
I know.

Dear Black Men,
I love you.
In case you don't hear it enough.

*Every day you're being told what you need to
work on,
What needs to be fixed.
Almost as if you're being punished for having a
dick.
That plus melanin? Your skin has to be thick.*

*I feel for you.
As someone who has encountered those that
misrepresent you,
I am here to say it is not your fault.
Just keep doing your best.
I wouldn't feel good if I didn't get this off my
chest.*

*It was a black man who revealed the essence of
unconditional love to me.
Not my father, not my brother, not my uncle, but
my friend.*

*So I am grateful therapy helped me to heal some
old wounds.
Because I healed the one that almost stopped me
from loving you.
A Black Man who lives in a world where he is
public enemy number one.
Yet he still finds it in his heart to trust me and
love.*

Hey there, Pretty girl

Hey there, pretty girl
your eyes remind me of something like mine.
It's like looking through the window and seeing
the sun while it shines.
It's like having a conversation with God, and
hearing that you are divine.
And the universe telling you that you are
resilient by design
One model, one of a kind
Because who else could beat death and continue
to climb
Who else could be a baby again and not lose
their mind?

Hey there, pretty girl, don't you ever forget
To keep your head up high every time you step
Unclench your jaw, relax your shoulders, stop
holding your breath
Feel the breeze on your skin
Act like it's the first time
And when it rains
don't complain
Because that signifies a new beginning
Wash away the past

So long to you bad vibes
I bid thee farewell

Hey there pretty girl, I see my story in your eyes
With every bad came a quarter of good
Yet you stand tall
As a warrior should
Isn't it amazing that the things you thought you
couldn't shake
No longer matter each morning you wake?

Because who cares
We're not sWeAtInG tHe sMaLL stuff
No, not anymore

Hey there pretty girl
You're gonna be okay for sure.

Boundaries

Setting boundaries isn't about you
        It's about me
I have a habit of overextending myself
Wanting to take the pain off your shoulders
Placing it on mine
Even though I have shit from 2006
that still gives my subconscious
The ick
I am not yet healed
        I am heal-ing
But I won't say a word about how I'm feeling
Not to you
My toxic trait is doing everything in my power
to keep those around me happy
My therapist would say I
People please
Because deep down I wish someone,
Anyone,
        would do the same for me
Make me a first thought
Make me a priority
Ask me how my day was
Because you genuinely care
it's not just a routine
        Tell me you love me

Make me feel seen
I just needed a friend
Who knows
          when I'm silently crying on the phone
When I put them on mute
To let my life unfold
Just for a few seconds
I want someone to truly know me
I thought that could've been you
              But I had to tell you No
I had to stand my ground
And your selfishness wouldn't allow you to
understand
                  That it wasn't about you
Setting boundaries
Doesn't mean "we beefing."
Holding you accountable doesn't make me your
enemy
You just don't like it when I put that mirror in
front of your face
                  But doing this makes me honest
      Doing that makes me real
    I won't apologize for setting

Boundaries

Arguments

15

Arguments don't make the love any less real
It doesn't change how you are the one person
I care about the most
It doesn't change that in a world full of lies,
grudges, thieves and corruption
You are still my happy place.

Daddy's Reason

From the chocolate in your eyes
To the copper on your skin

You give your dad a reason to wake up and be
proud

From your spirit of inquiry
To the hmm on your brow

You give your dad a reason to wake up and be
proud

From the love in your heart
To the songs in your soul

You give your dad a reason to wake up and be
proud

TRAPPED.

Trying to move
But my body won't allow it
My mind is making orders
Cheering on the parts that make me whole
Go! Go! Go!

Nothing.

Can you imagine
Waking up
And finding out you're stuck?
Stuck in your head
Stuck in your thoughts
While eyes you haven't seen since you were 12
or 16
Lay on you.
Adding to your hopelessness
Adding to your fear
That this is it.

The End is near.

I laid there, identical to a cucumber.
As my youth left me and returned.
The irony of it all.

Bed bound
Father says, "let me see you wiggle your toes."
I'm doing it, I'm doing it! In my head I would scream
Hoping he could hear me via telepathy.

My toes did nothing.

Have you ever communicated with just your eyes?
I'm not talking about that thing you do when you're pointing someone out to your friend.
I'm talking about a communication board
Blink once for them to keep going
Blink twice for them to stop at a letter so you can spell out a word.
Trying to form a sentence because the tubes down your throat won't permit you to be heard.

Have you ever laid frozen with a sheet at your waist?
Unable to cover your shoulders, your legs, your face?
So you lay there, sleepless through the night
Afraid that if you close your eyes, it would be your last time.

Pitch darkness,
An empty space

No relatives to take me across realms.
I assume I was just lost in consciousness

19

Not my time to go
But uncomfortable to stay
Because I was one with a vegetable
Yet constantly in pain

Have you ever been trapped in your body?

One phone call

I have a sister
She's a phone call away
Our bond,
Unbreakable

Best friend

I would step out into the ocean for you,
Knowing that I can't swim

I would cradle you,
Like a newborn to its mother's bosom

I would help you laugh your pain away,
To make you forget

I would listen to your stories for hours,
Admiring how you have no regrets

I would do for you,
Anything you would do for me

As two peas in a pod,
As the twin to your flame

As the one listed in your call log the most,
I'll always answer your call

Because you were always there for me,
Attitude and all.

Thank you best friend.

Still

Week night
Listening to Summer Walker
Feeling full
No emotions
Just still.

I'm okay with who I am
I'm okay with where I am
No expectations
No high hopes
Or bad dreams

I'm still

Listening to lyrics that resonate
Listening to Clear 2 and saying
Hmm
Why haven't my spirit guides talked to me so
explicitly?

I get downloads
I've always had the gift of *knowing*.
I've never been able to explain it
But I can read you well

You can lie, but what's in the dark must come to
light.

In this moment I feel full
Full of contentment
I'm honestly unbothered
Completely unperturbed
But don't get me wrong
I still have a care
A care in the world for what matters

I care for what's right
I care for my heart
I care for my surroundings
I care for my mind
My body
My soul
I care for my inner child
So I put in the outer work

In this moment I am still

Synonymous with water
I am it
It is me

Still full of courage
My voice has been set free
I say what I mean

I mean what I say
My throat chakra thanks me

I'm still

Still the one I believe in
Still learning
Still growing
Stagnancy scares me
So when I say I'm still
I mean in the sense of Progression.

I am still

Still the one who beat the odds
Still the school mom
Still Shan
Still Nika
Still Shannel
Still the fighter
Still the favorite

Still Shanika

Attachment Style

25

Since you left me
I fear
That the last time we spoke
Will be the last time you call
Empty spaces
Empty hearts
No one left to return

The Island

The apples are pear shaped,
Guineps are a tree climb away,

The music vibrates through your soul

Sunday mornings
All you need is your firewood and coal.

Go to church, sing their songs
Feel close to something

Iron your uniform
Pleat by pleat

Splash the water
Watch the steam

Ice cream would really make this day complete.
Great nut or grape nut
Whatever it's called
Doesn't really matter, we all say it wrong

Yeah that's the one.
Let the flavors orgasm onto your tongue

Let it melt away
Like your innocence

Laying somewhere
On the island

Consistent

I didn't grow up with comfort
I grew up with consistency

There was consistency in the way your voice
decibels would raise.
Consistency in how you disregarded my pain.
There was consistency in how much we moved
Consistency in my lack of roots
No childhood friend
Because I always had to say goodbye
And in their minds
I remain a faded memory
I hold on to them, when they don't even
remember me

There was consistency in me wishing someone
cared for me as much as I did them
Consistency in me yearning for
Attention
Preferably from you, but I'd take what I could
get

There was consistency in me pretending I had
superpowers
Watching Charmed

The power of three, Will set us free
But I had no second, had no third
Just the gift of writing and the willingness to
learn.

There was consistency in me feeling like a black
ewe
I don't look like him and I don't sound like you
My skin is different
My weight is different

There was consistency in you shaming me
With your talks of little girls, who could fit in
the cute outfits you wished you could buy me
But my size wouldn't allow it.

There was consistency in me hearing the word
fat.
Consistency in me crying because you called me
that
Consistency in my tears being the only words I
spoke
Consistency in wishing I was old enough to vote

Old enough to leave
Old enough to go
Consistency in me losing all hope

Consistency in me wishing I was UnAlive

Consistency in you never swallowing your pride

But today I have grown
I now know that it had nothing to do with me
It was projection
The only thing familiar to you was pain
So you made that my norm
You made that the only thing—consistent.

Questions For My Narcissist

Being honest is a superpower
I know you find this hard to believe

Because lies are easier for people to say
Lies help them to get their way

But at some point, the mask has to be taken off.
At some point, you have to look in the mirror

There's no lying your way out of your reflection.
No way to deny what you see

Are you happy with yourself?
You say yes, but you know the truth
You haven't made peace with what's inside
And lying is all you can do.

To recreate the past is a skill
Recounting events that never took place
Just so you can have something to talk about.
As you observe the looks on their face.

Aren't you tired of this facade?
I beg you, come out of your shell
You taught me lying was a sin

So why do you prefer to go to hell?

Or do you believe that you will be excused?
For the manipulation and dishonesty
Or the trauma you have caused me
Even though love is what you promised me

A Poem For My Daughter

I'd like to think you're proud of me.
And how far I've come.

Because I do it all for you.
Slowly creating the life that you deserve.

But sometimes this life comes with guilt.

I tend to the needs and emotions of
micro-humans every day.
Whenever they speak, I can't help but wonder if
this is something you would say.

Desperately wishing we could have a
conversation.
On my deathbed, I was hoping you'd visit me.
I just needed confirmation that you weren't mad
at me.

Because I was mad at myself.
Apparently, this is the second stage of grief.

But I have since turned my pain into purpose;
Would you believe
If I told you that your mom is a teacher now?

She uses a microphone so she doesn't speak too
loud
And her students call her extra,
but that's a compliment to her
She speaks to their minds and their souls
Asks thought provoking questions,
About their lives and their goals
When they feel broken,
She makes them feel whole
And in them all, she sees your beautiful soul.

She does this to honor you
Her beautiful baby girl, who would've been
turning seven.
Her only aspiration is to make you smile from
Heaven.
Oddly enough, I have a student by that name
Who makes me feel like the best human on
Earth
As I write this, I wonder if you've been
comforting me through her.

Gratitude

I am thankful for the breeze on my skin when I
step out in the morning.
We tend to take you for granted.
The sun and its rays are always appreciated by
me.
The water access that I have is something I
value.
Thank you to the birds and the bees.
For the oxygen I breathe with no complications,
I thank my lungs and the trees.
Thank you to my brain for the thoughts and
Ideas.
It feels so good to be creative.
Thank you to my voice, for being my
instrument, until I finally learn guitar.
Thank you to my bed, for being mine.
Thank you to my job, for the cash flow.
I am grateful for it all.
Thank you to my friends who check on me
everyday.
Loyalty is so hard to find.
Thank you to my heart for always being open.
Thank you to music for saving my life more than
once.
I am walking in my divine purpose.

Thank you.

Dear Daphene,

I wish to be bold like you,
And funny like Aaliyah
Polite like Firdaous
And well mannered like Mia

Loving like Zion
Caring like Gabe
Respectful like Brad
And humorous like Jay

Intelligent like Ashraff
Who always has the need to know
Yet quiet like Brandon whose voice still grows
Outspoken like Sharif, who means what he says
Or a tad like Tyree who has no regrets

I see you in me , I see me in you
I admire your persistence Zoey
And Jaleigha, you too!
You're so hardworking in all that you do

I want good memory like Carter, Jadiel and
Abdul
"Ms. Cuthbert's favorite colors are black, gold
and pink"

It rolls off your tongue, you don't have to think

I want determination like Ibrahim
Mastering two languages is no easy thing
I want to wear a smile on my face like Adelaide
I want to be proud like Malaysia when I earn
accolades

I want to be wise like Gracie, always knowing
what to say.
Consistent like Jayden—always with my hands
raised.
Bright like Starlyn, who beams from his rays.
Aware like Aryelle who knows there's a time and
a place.

I want to be kind like Mayreli—always showing
others love 🩶

Meeting all of you was God giving me a hug.